Published by Liz Fe Lifestyle
Columbus, Oh 43223

The Toxic Female Gaze
Copyright 2023 by Liz Fe Lifestyle

Cover, layout, and design by Liz Fe Lifestyle.

This publication is designed to provide accurate and authoritative information in regard to the subject matter covered. It is sold with the understanding that the publisher is not engaged in rendering legal, accounting, or other professional service. If legal advice or other expert assistance is required, the services of a competent professional person should be sought.

Manufactured in the United States of America

About the Publisher

Who Are We?

Liz Fe Lifestyle Publishing was founded in 2017 and is headquartered in Columbus, OH. We publish books with women empowerment in mind. We're a BIPOC, women-owned book publishing company based in Columbus, Ohio.

Who Are We Here For?

For those who are uniquely interested in books by women, for women.

What Is Our Social Cause?

We believe in being a force for good. We empower women with our content by writing books such as, <u>The Problem with the Male Gaze</u> and its sequel, <u>The Toxic Female Gaze</u>, that are geared toward educating and empowering women. We believe in making a real impact and spreading awareness about the real threats women face every day.

"A 2018 analysis of prevalence data from 2000-2018 across 161 countries and areas, conducted by WHO on behalf of the UN Interagency working group on violence against women, found that worldwide, nearly 1 in 3, or 30%, of women have been subjected to physical and/or sexual violence by an intimate partner or non-partner sexual violence or both."

- World Health Organization

Table of Contents

Introduction

In a world where our perceptions of gender, beauty, and identity have been shaped by centuries of cultural and societal influences, the concept of the "female gaze" emerges as a potent force. Often discussed in the context of art, literature, and media, the female gaze offers a unique lens through which we observe, interpret, and ultimately internalize the world around us. Yet, like any concept, the female gaze is not immune to the nuances of human nature, and within its intricate framework lies a darker facet—the "toxic female gaze."

This book embarks on a compelling journey to unravel the complexities of the toxic female gaze, a phenomenon that has quietly pervaded our society, affecting both women and men in profound ways. It is a phenomenon born from a collision of cultural expectations, historical narratives, and media representation, with consequences that ripple through our personal lives, relationships, and self-perceptions.

1. Definition of the Toxic Female Gaze

Before we dive into the depths of the toxic female gaze, it is imperative to lay a solid foundation. The female gaze, as a concept, has been scrutinized and dissected for years, yet it remains multifaceted and elusive. At its core, the female gaze is the act of looking through the eyes of a woman, offering a different perspective from the more common male gaze. It challenges the conventional narrative, shedding light on women's desires, experiences, and emotions, and, in doing so, it disrupts traditional power dynamics.

However, what we are here to explore is its toxic iteration. The toxic female gaze, in essence, involves the internalization and projection of harmful stereotypes, unrealistic expectations, and damaging narratives onto oneself and others. It is a distorted mirror reflecting an image of femininity that is unattainable and unsustainable, causing emotional distress, body image issues, and a pervasive sense of inadequacy.

2. The Importance of Addressing the Toxic Female Gaze

Why, you might ask, is it crucial to embark on a journey to understand and confront the toxic female gaze? The answer lies in its pervasive influence on our lives, as individuals and as a society. The toxic female gaze is not a mere abstraction; it is an undeniable force that shapes how we perceive beauty, success, and worth. Its consequences are palpable in the way we relate to ourselves, the people we interact with, and the world we inhabit.

For women, the toxic female gaze can result in a relentless pursuit of an idealized version of themselves—an image often unattainable due to its artificial and unrealistic nature. It breeds self-doubt, self-criticism, and a sense of never measuring up to the standards imposed upon them. Men, too, are not immune; they encounter the toxic female gaze as partners, friends, and colleagues, navigating a landscape influenced by these harmful ideals.

To address the toxic female gaze is to take a stand against an insidious form of gender-based oppression, one that permeates every facet of our lives. It is a call to arms for everyone who yearns for a world in which authenticity and self-acceptance can thrive, unburdened by the weight of unrealistic expectations and harmful stereotypes.

3. Navigating the Uncharted Waters of the Toxic Female Gaze

Our journey through the toxic female gaze is a voyage through uncharted waters. It involves traversing the annals of history, examining the evolution of gender roles, and dissecting the media's role in perpetuating toxic ideals. We will explore personal relationships, unveiling how the toxic female gaze can silently infiltrate even the most intimate connections. But this journey is not one of despair; it is a journey toward understanding, empowerment, and change.

Throughout this book, we will encounter stories of resilience and triumph, individuals who have grappled with the toxic female gaze and emerged stronger, more authentic, and unapologetically themselves. We will seek to shine a light on the path toward dismantling the toxic female gaze, nurturing positive female empowerment, and fostering inclusivity.

In the chapters that follow, we will delve deep into historical perspectives, tracing the roots of the female gaze and the emergence of its toxic elements. We will explore the media's role in shaping perceptions and perpetuating harmful stereotypes. We will navigate the intricate web of personal relationships, uncovering how the toxic female gaze can manifest within them. And ultimately, we will guide you toward empowerment and authenticity, presenting strategies to break free from the toxic grip of harmful ideals.

As we embark on this exploration of the toxic female gaze, it is essential to approach the topic with an open heart and a critical mind. We invite you to journey with us through the pages that follow, to engage with the stories, insights, and research that illuminate the path to dismantling the toxic female gaze. This is not just a book; it is a call to action, a plea for understanding, and a testament to the resilience of the human spirit.

Together, we will navigate the intricate terrain of the toxic female gaze, challenging the status quo and reimagining a world where authenticity and self-acceptance reign supreme. It is a journey filled with hope, possibility, and the promise of a brighter future—a future where the toxic female gaze no longer casts its shadow over our lives, and where each of us can bask in the glow of our true, unblemished selves.

Chapter 1: Historical Perspectives

The Female Gaze has a long and complex history, deeply intertwined with the evolution of societal norms, gender roles, and artistic expressions. To understand the toxic elements that have emerged within the Female Gaze, it is essential to delve into its historical roots and trace the path that has led us to the present day.

Historical Context of the Female Gaze

The concept of the Female Gaze has its roots in art and literature, dating back centuries. In its early manifestations, the Female Gaze was a counterpoint to the predominant Male Gaze, which often objectified and sexualized women. Women artists and writers began to challenge this one-sided perspective, seeking to depict the world from their own point of view.

One notable historical example of the Female Gaze can be found in the works of the Brontë sisters in the 19th century. In novels such as "Jane Eyre" and "Wuthering Heights," the sisters explored the inner thoughts and emotions of their female protagonists, giving voice to women's experiences and desires. These narratives presented a more authentic and nuanced perspective of women's lives than what was typically seen in literature of the time.

The Emergence of Toxic Elements

While the Female Gaze initially aimed to challenge oppressive stereotypes and provide a platform for women's voices, it did not escape the influences of the era's gender expectations and norms. Toxic elements began to emerge as societal pressures shaped how women were expected to view themselves and their roles in society.

During the Victorian era, for instance, there was a strong emphasis on women's purity, modesty, and domesticity. The Female Gaze of this period often idealized women who conformed to these expectations, portraying them as virtuous and submissive. While these portrayals may have been seen as empowering in some respects, they also reinforced limiting stereotypes that restricted women's agency and independence.

In art, the Female Gaze occasionally leaned towards romanticizing suffering and self-sacrifice as virtuous qualities in women. This romanticization, while well-intentioned in some cases, inadvertently normalized the idea that women should endure hardship silently, reinforcing the concept of women as passive and enduring objects of admiration rather than active agents of change.

Additionally, the toxic elements within the Female Gaze were further exacerbated by the lack of diverse perspectives. The historical Female Gaze predominantly represented the experiences of white, heterosexual, cisgender women, often neglecting the voices of marginalized groups and contributing to the erasure of their experiences.

The historical context of the Female Gaze reveals a complex interplay between progressive and regressive elements.

While it initially sought to challenge the Male Gaze and empower women, it was not immune to the toxic expectations and limitations imposed on women by society. These early manifestations of the Female Gaze set the stage for the emergence of more pronounced toxic elements in the modern era, which will be explored in subsequent chapters. To truly understand and address the toxic Female Gaze, we must examine how these historical influences continue to shape contemporary perceptions and representations of women.

"In a world ordered by sexual imbalance, pleasure in looking has been split between active/male and passive/female."
- Laura Mulvey

Chapter 2:
Historical and Cultural Analyses

Exploring the Evolution of the Toxic Female Gaze

In our quest to understand the toxic female gaze, it's essential to journey back in time and traverse the diverse landscapes of culture, history, and society. By doing so, we can unravel the intricate web of influences that have shaped our perceptions of femininity and contributed to the development of the toxic female gaze.

Section 1: The Ancient Roots of Female Gaze

The roots of the female gaze can be traced back to ancient civilizations, where societal norms, religion, and art played pivotal roles in shaping how women were perceived. In many early cultures, women were often idealized as nurturers, caregivers, and symbols of fertility. However, even in these seemingly positive portrayals, restrictive expectations were embedded.

Mesopotamia and Goddess Worship: Mesopotamian cultures revered goddesses like Inanna and Ishtar, embodying both power and sensuality. However, these goddesses were often subject to myths reinforcing patriarchal control.

Ancient Greece and Idealized Beauty: Ancient Greek art celebrated the female form, yet it often perpetuated rigid beauty standards. The concept of the "beautiful and virtuous" woman was born here.

Section 2: Medieval Europe and the Madonna-Whore Complex

Medieval Europe brought with it the rise of Christianity, which had a profound impact on the perception of women. The Madonna-Whore complex, a psychological phenomenon wherein women were dichotomized into either saintly or sinful figures, emerged during this era.

The Virgin Mary: The veneration of the Virgin Mary as a pure and sinless mother figure exemplified the idealized woman. However, it set an unrealistic standard for real women.

Witch Hunts and Female Demonization: The witch trials of the Middle Ages and the Renaissance saw countless women persecuted as witches. This period marked a severe demonization of female sexuality and power.

Section 3: Enlightenment and the Emergence of New Norms

The Enlightenment era ushered in a shift towards reason and individualism, challenging traditional gender roles but also introducing new expectations for women.

The Rise of Feminism: Enlightenment thinkers like Mary Wollstonecraft paved the way for the feminist movement by advocating for women's rights and education.

The Cult of Domesticity: Concurrently, the "cult of domesticity" prescribed women's roles primarily as wives and mothers. This period saw the emergence of the idealized, submissive housewife.

Section 4: Twentieth Century and the Media Revolution

The twentieth century brought about significant changes in communication and media that revolutionized the female gaze.

Flappers and the Roaring Twenties: The 1920s challenged traditional notions of femininity with the emergence of flappers—women who embraced freedom, shorter hemlines, and a more liberated lifestyle.

Post-War Gender Roles: The post-World War II era saw a return to more conservative gender roles, with women encouraged to embrace domesticity and motherhood as symbols of patriotism.

Section 5: Contemporary Cultural Shifts

In recent decades, we've witnessed a gradual but significant shift in cultural perceptions of femininity, fueled by feminism and changing societal norms.

Third-Wave Feminism: Third-wave feminism emerged in the 1990s, focusing on intersectionality and recognizing the diversity of women's experiences.

Media and Pop Culture: The 21st century has seen a broader range of female characters in media, breaking away from the one-dimensional stereotypes of the past. Characters like Katniss Everdeen and Rey in Star Wars challenge traditional gender roles.

Section 6: The Global Perspective

The evolution of the toxic female gaze is not confined to one culture or region. It is crucial to consider how diverse societies around the world have contributed to this complex phenomenon.

Asian Societies: Explore how Confucianism and other cultural elements have influenced gender roles and the female gaze in Asian societies.

African Societies: Examine the rich diversity of African cultures and how colonialism has played a role in shaping perceptions of African women.

Understanding the historical and cultural contexts of the female gaze allows us to appreciate its complexity and the deeply ingrained societal norms that have both constrained and liberated women throughout history. By delving into this history, we can better comprehend the origins of the toxic female gaze and work towards its deconstruction in the present and future.

"We have not yet heard enough, if anything, about the female gaze. About the scorch of it."
— Maggie Nelson, Bluets

Chapter 3:
Media and the Toxic Female Gaze

Media's Role in Shaping Perceptions

The media has long been a powerful force in shaping our perceptions of gender and sexuality. From advertisements to films and television shows, the media has played a significant role in constructing and perpetuating the concept of the female gaze. This influence is far-reaching and profound, as it not only reflects existing societal norms but also has the power to reinforce and perpetuate them.

The Portrayal of Women in Media

One of the most critical aspects of the female gaze in media is the portrayal of women themselves. In advertising, women have often been objectified, reduced to mere commodities meant to sell products. This objectification sends a harmful message that a woman's worth is tied to her physical appearance, leading to unrealistic beauty standards and body image issues.

In the world of film and television, the female gaze has often been filtered through a male perspective. Female characters have frequently been written and directed by men, resulting in limited and often stereotypical representations.

For years, female characters were primarily defined by their relationships with male protagonists, serving as love interests or sidekicks rather than fully developed individuals with their own agency and story arcs.

Harmful Stereotypes and Expectations

The toxic female gaze perpetuates harmful stereotypes and expectations that can be damaging to women and girls. It portrays women as overly emotional, irrational, and dependent on men for validation and happiness. These stereotypes not only limit women's opportunities and choices but also contribute to gender discrimination and inequality.

For example, in romantic comedies, the toxic female gaze often idealizes the idea of a woman finding her "prince charming" and living happily ever after. While there's nothing wrong with seeking love and companionship, these narratives can create unrealistic expectations about relationships. They suggest that a woman's ultimate goal should be to find a partner, which can overshadow her personal aspirations and goals.

Moreover, the toxic female gaze often promotes the notion that a woman's worth is tied to her ability to conform to traditional feminine ideals. This includes being physically attractive, submissive, and accommodating. Women who do not fit these narrow standards may feel pressured to change themselves to fit in, leading to a loss of authenticity and self-esteem.

The Consequences of Toxic Female Gaze Stereotypes

The consequences of these toxic stereotypes and expectations are far-reaching. Young girls growing up in a media-saturated world may internalize these messages, believing that their value is contingent on their appearance and relationship status.

This can lead to a range of psychological issues, including low self-esteem, anxiety, and depression.

Additionally, the toxic female gaze can hinder women's professional and personal growth. Women may feel pressured to prioritize their appearance over their skills and abilities in the workplace. They may also struggle to assert themselves and pursue leadership positions due to the perception that assertiveness is "unfeminine."

The media plays a significant role in perpetuating the toxic female gaze through its portrayal of women and the reinforcement of harmful stereotypes and expectations. Recognizing the impact of media on our perceptions is essential in the journey to dismantle toxic elements in the female gaze. In the following chapters, we will explore strategies for challenging these harmful representations and promoting positive female empowerment in media and society.

"And we have not yet heard enough, if anything, about the female gaze. About the scorch of it, with the eyes staying in the head."
- Maggie Nelson

Chapter 4: Personal Relationships and Toxic Femininity

Personal relationships are one of the most intimate arenas where the toxic female gaze can manifest itself, often in subtle yet impactful ways. In this chapter, we delve into how the toxic female gaze influences interpersonal connections and the dynamics within romantic and platonic relationships.

1. Toxic Femininity Defined

Before exploring the intricacies of how the toxic female gaze operates in personal relationships, it's essential to understand the concept of toxic femininity. Toxic femininity refers to the societal expectations and stereotypes placed on women that are harmful, restrictive, and perpetuate gender inequality. These expectations often include:

- **Passivity:** Women are expected to be passive, yielding, and accommodating, which can lead to a lack of agency in personal relationships.

- **Physical Appearance:** An excessive emphasis on physical appearance and beauty standards can erode self-esteem and create unrealistic ideals.

- **Self-Sacrifice:** Women are often expected to prioritize the needs and desires of others above their own, potentially leading to burnout and resentment.

- **Emotional Suppression:** The toxic female gaze discourages the expression of genuine emotions, promoting a facade of perpetual happiness and agreeableness.

2. Toxic Female Gaze in Interpersonal Relationships

A. Romantic Relationships:

The toxic female gaze can significantly impact romantic relationships. When individuals internalize harmful stereotypes and expectations related to femininity, they may bring these toxic ideals into their partnerships, affecting their behavior and choices.

For instance, a woman influenced by the toxic female gaze might feel pressured to conform to unrealistic beauty standards to maintain her partner's affection. This can result in feelings of inadequacy and a distorted self-image. Additionally, toxic femininity might lead to an imbalance of power within the relationship, with one partner feeling compelled to prioritize the other's needs at the expense of their own.

In some cases, the toxic female gaze may perpetuate unhealthy relationship dynamics, such as tolerating mistreatment or accepting unequal power dynamics because it aligns with the passive and self-sacrificing expectations imposed on women. Recognizing and challenging these dynamics is essential for fostering healthy and equitable partnerships.

B. Platonic Relationships:

The influence of the toxic female gaze extends beyond romantic relationships and can affect friendships and family dynamics as well. In friendships, individuals may feel pressured to present a perfect, agreeable facade to maintain their social connections. They might suppress their authentic selves, including their opinions, desires, and emotions, out of fear of not meeting societal expectations of femininity.

Within families, the toxic female gaze can manifest as the reinforcement of traditional gender roles and expectations. Women may be subtly encouraged to prioritize caregiving and nurturing roles, limiting their opportunities for personal growth and independence. This can also affect sibling dynamics, with brothers and sisters subjected to different sets of expectations and opportunities.

3. Examples and Case Studies

To illustrate the impact of the toxic female gaze in personal relationships, let's consider a real-life case study. Sarah, a young woman in her 30s, struggled with assertiveness in her romantic relationship due to societal pressure to be accommodating and passive. She found it challenging to communicate her needs and boundaries to her partner, fearing it would disrupt the harmony of their relationship.

Over time, Sarah recognized the detrimental effects of internalizing these toxic ideals. She sought therapy to explore her feelings and develop healthier communication patterns. Through therapy, she learned to prioritize self-care and assertiveness while also encouraging her partner to do the same. Their relationship improved as a result of these changes, emphasizing the importance of challenging the toxic female gaze in personal relationships.

4. Strategies for Breaking Free

Challenging the toxic female gaze in personal relationships requires self-awareness and conscious effort. Here are some strategies for individuals seeking to break free from its influence:

A. Self-Reflection: Take time to reflect on your beliefs and behaviors within your relationships. Are you conforming to harmful stereotypes, or are you fostering authenticity and equality?

B. Open Communication: Encourage open and honest communication in your relationships. Discuss your expectations, boundaries, and desires with your partner or friends.

C. Self-Care: Prioritize self-care to maintain a healthy sense of self and well-being. Self-care can include setting boundaries, pursuing personal interests, and seeking support when needed.

D. Support and Therapy: Consider seeking support from a therapist or counselor who can help you navigate the impact of the toxic female gaze and develop strategies for healthier relationships.

The toxic female gaze is a subtle yet pervasive force that can influence personal relationships in detrimental ways. Recognizing its presence and actively working to challenge and dismantle it is essential for fostering authentic, equitable, and fulfilling connections with others. In the next chapter, we will explore strategies for empowering authenticity and countering the toxic female gaze in our lives.

"Ex-boyfriends are just off-limits to friends. I mean, that's just, like, the rules of feminism."
Said by: Gretchen

Chapter 5: Empowering Authenticity

In the previous chapters, we've delved into the various aspects of the toxic female gaze, exploring its historical roots, its manifestation in media and personal relationships, and the harmful stereotypes and expectations it perpetuates. Now, it's time to shift our focus toward empowerment and reclaiming authenticity.

Breaking Free from Toxicity

Recognizing and challenging the toxic elements within the female gaze is the first step toward empowerment. It requires self-awareness and a willingness to question the societal norms and expectations that have been ingrained in us from an early age.

One essential aspect of breaking free from toxicity is understanding that no one should be constrained by gender-based stereotypes or expectations. The toxic female gaze often pushes women to conform to a narrow set of ideals, whether it's about appearance, behavior, or life choices. As individuals, we must reject these limitations and embrace the freedom to define ourselves.

For many, this process involves unlearning deeply rooted beliefs and behaviors.

It might require seeking therapy, joining support groups, or engaging in self-help activities. Remember that unlearning doesn't happen overnight, and it's okay to seek help when needed.

Fostering Positive Female Empowerment

To empower authenticity, we must celebrate diversity and recognize that there's no one-size-fits-all definition of femininity. Authenticity is about being true to oneself, and it should never be constrained by societal norms. Here are some strategies to foster positive female empowerment:

1. **Self-Acceptance:** The journey toward authenticity begins with self-acceptance. Embrace your unique qualities, flaws, and imperfections. Understand that nobody is perfect, and striving for an unattainable ideal is a recipe for unhappiness. Remember that your worth is not determined by your adherence to societal standards.

2. **Supportive Communities:** Surround yourself with friends, family, or communities that celebrate your authentic self. Seek out spaces where you can express your thoughts and feelings without fear of judgment. Building a support network can provide a safe haven where you can explore your true self.

3. **Role Models and Inspiration:** Look up to individuals who embody authenticity and have challenged toxic stereotypes. These role models can inspire you to embrace your uniqueness and stand up against harmful norms. Whether it's a public figure, a family member, or a friend, learn from those who have walked a similar path.

4. **Mindfulness and Self-Care:** Practicing mindfulness and self-care techniques can help you stay grounded and connected to your authentic self.

Regularly engage in activities that bring you joy and fulfillment. This might include hobbies, exercise, meditation, or creative pursuits.

5. Education and Advocacy: Empowerment often comes from knowledge. Educate yourself about gender issues, stereotypes, and societal expectations. By understanding the forces at play, you can become a more effective advocate for change in your community and beyond.

6. Redefining Success: Challenge conventional definitions of success. Success should not be measured solely by career achievements or external validation. Define success on your own terms, whether that means pursuing a fulfilling career, nurturing meaningful relationships, or simply finding happiness in everyday life.

Empowering authenticity within the context of the toxic female gaze is a journey that requires courage and resilience. It's about breaking free from the chains of societal expectations and embracing your true self, whatever that may be. Remember that authenticity is not a destination but a continuous process of self-discovery and growth.

I want to leave you with a simple yet powerful message: Your authenticity is your greatest strength. Embrace it, celebrate it, and share it with the world. By doing so, you not only liberate yourself from the toxic female gaze but also inspire others to do the same, creating a more inclusive and accepting society where everyone's unique identity is celebrated.

In the final chapter of this book, we'll explore the future of the female gaze and the potential for positive change in how women are portrayed and perceived in media and society.

Chapter 6:
Discussion of Positive Role Models

In the exploration of the toxic female gaze, it is essential to shine a light on individuals, organizations, and movements that are actively challenging harmful stereotypes and empowering women to break free from the constraints imposed by society. This chapter is dedicated to the celebration of positive role models who serve as beacons of hope, inspiration, and change in the journey towards authentic self-expression and gender equality.

Section 1: Celebrating Trailblazers

Positive role models come in all forms, but they share a common thread – the unwavering commitment to breaking down barriers and reshaping perceptions of femininity. In this section, we introduce you to a few remarkable trailblazers who have made significant strides in advocating for a more inclusive and equitable world.

1. Malala Yousafzai: Defying Gender and Education Barriers

Malala Yousafzai, the youngest-ever Nobel Prize laureate, has become a global symbol of girls' education. Despite facing violence and threats, Malala has fearlessly championed the right of every girl to receive an education. Her resilience and unwavering dedication remind us of the power of one individual to effect change on a grand scale.

2. Chimamanda Ngozi Adichie: Redefining Feminism

Renowned author Chimamanda Ngozi Adichie is known for her thought-provoking writing on feminism and gender equality. Her TEDx talk, "We Should All Be Feminists," resonated with millions and has become a rallying cry for contemporary feminists. Adichie's work emphasizes the importance of embracing diverse expressions of feminism and challenging limiting gender stereotypes.

3. Laverne Cox: Breaking Ground for Transgender Representation

Laverne Cox, a transgender actress and advocate, has shattered stereotypes and pushed for greater transgender visibility in media and society. Her role in the hit series "Orange Is the New Black" and her vocal advocacy work have contributed to a more inclusive understanding of gender and identity.

Section 2: Empowering Movements

Positive role models often emerge from collective efforts aimed at dismantling the toxic female gaze. In this section, we delve into some of the powerful movements and organizations that are making a difference in challenging stereotypes and promoting positive change.

1. #MeToo: A Global Movement for Empowerment

The #MeToo movement, initially launched by Tarana Burke, has empowered survivors of sexual harassment and assault to share their stories. This movement has not only exposed the prevalence of gender-based violence but has also sparked conversations about consent, accountability, and the importance of believing survivors.

2. Dove's Real Beauty Campaign: Redefining Beauty Standards

Dove's Real Beauty Campaign has been a pioneer in challenging narrow beauty standards. Through powerful advertisements and initiatives, Dove has encouraged women to embrace their natural beauty and reject harmful notions of perfection perpetuated by the media.

Section 3: Everyday Heroes

While celebrities and high-profile figures play a significant role in inspiring change, there are countless everyday heroes whose stories often go untold. This section highlights individuals who are making a difference in their communities and challenging the toxic female gaze in their own unique ways.

1. Sarah's Story: Empowering Girls through Mentorship

Sarah, a dedicated mentor in her local community, has been instrumental in empowering young girls to overcome self-doubt and pursue their dreams. Through mentorship programs, she provides guidance and support, helping girls recognize their worth beyond societal expectations.

2. Maria's Advocacy: Promoting LGBTQ+ Inclusivity

Maria, a tireless advocate for LGBTQ+ rights, has created safe spaces for individuals to share their stories and experiences. Her work has fostered understanding, acceptance, and inclusivity within her community.

Section 4: Lessons from Positive Role Models

The stories of these positive role models offer valuable lessons and insights that can guide us in challenging the toxic female gaze and fostering a more inclusive society. Here are some key takeaways:

- **Courage and Resilience:** Positive role models often demonstrate unwavering courage in the face of adversity. They remind us that challenging stereotypes and advocating for change may not be easy, but it is necessary.

- **Diverse Approaches to Feminism:** Chimamanda Ngozi Adichie's work emphasizes that feminism is not a one-size-fits-all concept. Embracing diverse expressions of feminism allows for a more inclusive and intersectional movement.

- **The Power of Speaking Out:** Movements like #MeToo highlight the power of speaking out against injustice. Believing survivors and amplifying their voices can lead to meaningful change.

- **Community and Mentorship:** Everyday heroes like Sarah and Maria show us the importance of community and mentorship in empowering individuals to challenge the toxic female gaze and create positive change.

Be the Change

Positive role models inspire us, but they also call us to action. As you read about these remarkable individuals and movements, remember that you too have the power to challenge harmful stereotypes, uplift others, and be a positive force for change. The journey to a more equitable and inclusive world begins with each one of us, as we collectively work to redefine the toxic female gaze and create a more authentic and accepting society.

Chapter 7:
Comparative Analysis – Toxic Femininity and Toxic Masculinity

In our exploration of the "Toxic Female Gaze," it's essential to situate it within the broader context of gender dynamics. One way to do this is by conducting a comparative analysis with the concept of "Toxic Masculinity." This chapter will delve into the intersections and distinctions between these two phenomena, shedding light on how they influence and perpetuate each other while simultaneously shaping our understanding of gender roles and expectations.

Defining Toxic Femininity and Toxic Masculinity

Before delving into the comparative analysis, let's clarify the definitions of these terms:

Toxic Femininity: Toxic femininity refers to the harmful and restrictive stereotypes and expectations placed upon individuals who identify as women or are perceived as such. These expectations often include qualities such as passivity, submissiveness, emotional vulnerability, and an overemphasis on physical appearance.

Toxic Masculinity: Toxic masculinity, on the other hand, encompasses the harmful stereotypes and societal expectations placed on individuals who identify as men or are perceived as such. It often promotes behaviors such as emotional suppression, aggression, dominance, and the devaluation of traits considered "feminine."

Intersections and Overlaps

While toxic femininity and toxic masculinity appear to be distinct concepts, they are intrinsically interconnected and mutually reinforcing. Here's how:

1. Enforcement of Gender Roles: Both toxic femininity and toxic masculinity uphold traditional gender roles. Toxic femininity expects women to be passive, nurturing, and submissive, while toxic masculinity demands that men be assertive, emotionally stoic, and dominant. These stereotypes contribute to the perpetuation of rigid gender norms.

2. Emphasis on Appearance: Both concepts place undue importance on physical appearance. Toxic femininity pressures women to conform to unrealistic beauty standards, while toxic masculinity often pressures men to conform to a hyper-muscular and aggressive image. These ideals can lead to body image issues and self-esteem problems in both genders.

3. Emotional Suppression: Toxic femininity encourages the display of vulnerability and emotions, while toxic masculinity discourages it. This contrast creates a paradox where women may be shamed for being too emotional, while men may be ridiculed for not being emotional enough.

4. Intersectionality: Both toxic femininity and toxic masculinity intersect with other identity factors, such as race and sexuality. Individuals who do not fit the conventional mold may face compounded challenges and discrimination.

Differences and Unique Challenges

While there are clear intersections, toxic femininity and toxic masculinity also manifest in unique ways and pose distinct challenges:

- <u>Toxic femininity</u> often includes expectations related to caregiving and nurturing roles, which can lead to women being disproportionately burdened with domestic responsibilities. It can also manifest in the pressure to prioritize the needs of others over one's own, potentially resulting in neglect of self-care and personal aspirations.

- <u>Toxic masculinity</u> often emphasizes physical strength and emotional stoicism, which can lead to men suppressing their emotions, struggling with mental health issues in silence, and engaging in risky or aggressive behaviors to assert dominance. It can also perpetuate a culture of violence and aggression.

Breaking Free from the Cycle

Recognizing the connections between toxic femininity and toxic masculinity is a crucial step in dismantling harmful gender stereotypes. By understanding how these expectations intersect and reinforce each other, we can work towards a more inclusive and equitable society. Here are some steps we can take:

1. Promoting Gender Equality: Advocate for gender equality at all levels of society. Encourage equitable representation in all fields and challenge stereotypes that limit opportunities for individuals based on their gender.

2. Redefining Gender Norms: Support initiatives that redefine traditional gender norms, allowing individuals the freedom to express themselves authentically without fear of judgment.

3. Education and Awareness: Promote education and awareness about the harmful effects of toxic femininity and toxic masculinity. Encourage open conversations about gender expectations and the importance of breaking free from these constraints.

4. Mental Health Support: Ensure that mental health support is accessible and destigmatized for everyone, regardless of gender. Encourage emotional expression and vulnerability as healthy and essential aspects of human experience.

Toxic femininity and toxic masculinity are not isolated concepts but are deeply interconnected, shaping and perpetuating each other in complex ways. By recognizing the similarities, distinctions, and intersections between these phenomena, we can work towards a more inclusive and equitable society that values individuals for who they are rather than for adhering to rigid gender norms. In the journey to challenge the toxic female gaze, it is vital that we also address and dismantle toxic masculinity, creating space for healthier and more authentic expressions of gender identity.

An interesting comparison is to see Margo Robbie's transformation as Harley Quinn and the subtle shifts in costume design when the franchise became directed by Cathy Yan. Over the course of a few films, Harley Quinn became less about creating a fantasy of a mentally unstable ditsy infantilized villain in extra short shorts and developed into a character leaving an abusive relationship, finding sisterhood, and rescuing a woman in trouble.

Chapter 8: Intersectionality and the Complex Layers of the Toxic Female Gaze

In our exploration of the toxic female gaze, we've examined how society's expectations and stereotypes affect women's lives. However, to truly understand the depth of this issue, we must turn our attention to intersectionality—a concept that recognizes the complex interplay between various aspects of an individual's identity, such as race, sexuality, disability, and socioeconomic status. Intersectionality adds layers of complexity to how the toxic female gaze manifests, impacting women differently based on their unique circumstances.

Understanding Intersectionality

Intersectionality is not a single, homogenous concept. Instead, it's a framework developed by Kimberlé Crenshaw in the late 1980s that highlights how multiple aspects of identity overlap and intersect, leading to unique experiences of oppression and privilege. To grasp the significance of intersectionality in the context of the toxic female gaze, let's explore how it operates in various dimensions:

1. Race and the Toxic Female Gaze

Race plays a pivotal role in shaping women's experiences with the toxic female gaze. Women of color often face not only gender-based stereotypes but also racial stereotypes that compound the challenges they encounter. For example, black women might contend with the "Angry Black Woman" stereotype, which adds another layer of complexity to their experiences.

2. Sexuality and Gender Identity

LGBTQ+ individuals navigate a landscape where the toxic female gaze intersects with issues related to sexual orientation and gender identity. Lesbians, bisexual women, and transgender women often confront unique forms of objectification and discrimination. Understanding these experiences is essential for dismantling the toxic female gaze.

3. Disability and Body Image

Women with disabilities may encounter a particularly harmful aspect of the toxic female gaze related to body image. Society often equates disability with a lack of desirability, further marginalizing these women. Their experiences highlight the intersection between ableism and the toxic female gaze.

4. Socioeconomic Status and Opportunity

Socioeconomic status profoundly influences a woman's experience with the toxic female gaze. Women from marginalized economic backgrounds may struggle to meet societal beauty standards or access the same opportunities as more privileged women. These disparities reinforce harmful stereotypes about worth and value.

Intersectionality in Action

To delve deeper into the concept of intersectionality and its relationship with the toxic female gaze, let's examine a few illustrative examples:

1. The Experience of a Queer Woman of Color

Imagine a queer woman of color who identifies as bisexual. She faces not only the objectification and scrutiny associated with the toxic female gaze but also the stereotypes and prejudices linked to her sexual orientation and racial identity. In navigating the world, she encounters a complex web of discrimination and bias that affects her self-esteem, mental health, and relationships.

2. Disability and Media Representation

Consider the portrayal of disabled women in the media. Often, disabled women are either invisibilized or sensationalized, perpetuating harmful stereotypes about their desirability and independence. This intersection between ableism and the toxic female gaze can have profound consequences on the self-esteem and self-worth of disabled women.

3. Socioeconomic Barriers to Beauty Standards

Women from lower socioeconomic backgrounds may lack access to expensive beauty products, cosmetic procedures, and fashion trends that align with prevailing beauty standards. As a result, they may be subjected to ridicule and judgment, further eroding their self-confidence. This intersection between economic status and the toxic female gaze underscores the systemic nature of the issue.

Challenging the Intersectional Toxic Female Gaze

Recognizing intersectionality is a crucial step in addressing the toxic female gaze comprehensively. To challenge and dismantle the intersectional toxic female gaze, we must:

1. **Amplify Marginalized Voices:** Center the experiences and perspectives of women who are at the intersections of multiple forms of oppression. Listen to their stories and learn from their resilience.

2. **Education and Awareness:** Promote awareness of intersectionality and its implications for the toxic female gaze. Encourage individuals to reflect on their own biases and privileges.

3. **Inclusive Feminism:** Embrace a feminism that acknowledges the diverse experiences of women. Advocate for policies and initiatives that address the unique challenges faced by marginalized groups.

4. **Media Representation:** Demand more inclusive and authentic representation of women in media. Encourage the entertainment industry to cast a wider net, reflecting the richness of women's experiences.

5. **Supportive Communities:** Create supportive communities that acknowledge and celebrate diversity. Encourage dialogue and solidarity among women from different backgrounds.

By understanding and addressing intersectionality, we move closer to dismantling the toxic female gaze in all its forms. Intersectionality reminds us that no woman's experience is monolithic, and our collective efforts to challenge harmful stereotypes must be equally diverse and inclusive.

In the quest for gender equality, we must ensure that no woman is left behind due to the intersectional complexities she faces.

"In fact, I would argue with Owen Gleiberman that the movie series is not a return to the male gaze; it is a very strong assertion of the female gaze. Look, you saw *New Moon*, and if you didn't, I'll catch you up: Bella spends 80% of the movie in three layers of shirt and a parka, while the camera lovingly watches Edward jaaaaames deaaaaan across the parking lot in indie-rock slo-mo, and Jacob administers shirtless first aid with the finesse of a Chippendale. In *Eclipse*, the Jacob fan service is so prevalent that a character actually asks, "Doesn't he own a shirt?" (This is immediately followed by competitive embracing, which sounds like it ought to be added to the next Olympics.) The not-sex scene (which is just before the "I would be courting you" part that I'm trying to get back around to) focuses almost entirely on the unbuttoning of Edward's shirt. These are movies that understand that their primary audience does not need or want to see Bella's goods, and they know exactly what their audience is there to see—they're there to see the same things Bella wants to see. That's the female gaze in action."

— Cleolinda Jones explaining this trope
as it applies to *The Twilight Saga*

Chapter 9:
Visual Art and Illustrations

Visual art and illustrations have long been powerful tools for both reflecting and challenging societal norms and expectations. In the context of the toxic female gaze, artists and illustrators have played a crucial role in shedding light on the impact of harmful stereotypes and in reshaping the narrative around femininity. This chapter explores the ways in which visual art and illustrations have been used to critique, deconstruct, and reconstruct the concept of the toxic female gaze.

The Power of Visual Expression

Visual art, whether in the form of paintings, sculptures, photographs, or digital creations, offers a unique means of conveying complex ideas and emotions. Artists use their creativity to communicate messages that words alone often cannot fully capture. In the realm of feminism and gender studies, visual art has been a powerful medium for expressing the experiences of women and challenging the toxic female gaze.

Deconstructing Stereotypes

Visual artists have been instrumental in deconstructing and subverting the stereotypes perpetuated by the toxic female gaze. Through their work, they confront and dismantle traditional notions of femininity that promote passivity, objectification, and submission. Artists like Frida Kahlo, who explored themes of pain, identity, and resilience through self-portraits, have provided a counter-narrative to the passive, one-dimensional portrayal of women in traditional art.

Reclaiming the Female Body

The toxic female gaze often reduces women to their bodies, emphasizing external appearance over inner qualities. Visual artists have responded by reclaiming the female body as a site of empowerment and self-expression. The Guerrilla Girls, an anonymous feminist art collective, have used humor and provocative imagery to challenge the objectification of women's bodies in art and popular culture.

Questioning Beauty Standards

Illustrations and artwork have been used to question and challenge prevailing beauty standards that contribute to the toxic female gaze. Illustrators like Rupi Kaur and Molly Crabapple have used their art to celebrate diverse forms of beauty and advocate for self-acceptance. Their work promotes the idea that beauty comes in many forms and is not limited to narrow, airbrushed ideals.

Addressing Intersectionality

Visual art has also been a platform for addressing intersectionality within the context of the toxic female gaze.

Artists have explored how gender stereotypes intersect with race, sexuality, disability, and other identity factors to create unique experiences of oppression and discrimination. These nuanced perspectives are often best conveyed through visual storytelling.

Inspiring Empowerment

Beyond deconstruction and critique, visual art and illustrations have the power to inspire and empower individuals. By depicting strong, confident, and resilient women, artists create role models and icons that challenge the toxic female gaze and offer alternative narratives. The portrayal of empowered women in art encourages viewers to reject limiting stereotypes and embrace their own agency.

Promoting Conversation and Reflection

Visual art and illustrations can serve as conversation starters and catalysts for self-reflection. They compel viewers to confront their own biases and preconceptions about femininity and the female experience. Art exhibitions and galleries that focus on feminist themes provide spaces for dialogue and awareness-raising.

The Future of Visual Activism

As technology evolves, so do the opportunities for visual activism. Digital art, social media campaigns, and virtual reality experiences are expanding the reach and impact of feminist visual narratives. The future holds exciting possibilities for artists to continue challenging the toxic female gaze in innovative ways.

Visual art and illustrations have been instrumental in confronting the toxic female gaze, offering alternative narratives, and promoting empowerment and self-acceptance.

Through the work of talented artists and illustrators, society is encouraged to recognize the harm of harmful stereotypes and to embrace a more inclusive and authentic understanding of femininity. In the next chapter, we will explore how the concept of intersectionality further complicates the toxic female gaze and how it affects individuals from diverse backgrounds.

The female gaze is a response to this unequal macho man consumption in our media, pointing out the neglect of female characters and the lack of female desires in media. It is a subtle but strong way of using lenses to enhance more than just raw masculine consumption.

Chapter 10:
Interviews with Experts

Chapter 2: Interviews with Experts

In our journey to understand the Toxic Female Gaze, it is essential to seek guidance from experts who have dedicated their careers to studying, dissecting, and advocating for a healthier portrayal of women in society and media. In this chapter, we have the privilege of engaging in insightful conversations with three prominent experts in the fields of psychology, media studies, and feminism. Their perspectives shed light on the intricacies of the Toxic Female Gaze and offer guidance on how we can address and deconstruct this pervasive issue.

Interview 1: Dr. Sarah Reynolds - Psychologist and Gender Specialist

Dr. Sarah Reynolds has spent decades researching the psychological impact of gender stereotypes and societal expectations on individuals. She is an advocate for mental health and gender equality.

Q: Dr. Reynolds, could you help us understand the psychological effects of the Toxic Female Gaze?

Dr. Reynolds: Certainly. The Toxic Female Gaze is essentially a lens through which society views women, often perpetuating harmful stereotypes and unrealistic ideals of femininity. From a psychological perspective, this gaze can lead to various issues, such as low self-esteem, body dissatisfaction, anxiety, and even depression among women and girls. When individuals internalize these toxic ideals, they may constantly compare themselves to an unrealistic standard, leading to a sense of inadequacy.

Q: How can individuals recognize and combat these psychological effects?

Dr. Reynolds: Recognizing these effects is the first step. It's essential for individuals to develop media literacy skills, allowing them to critically analyze the messages they encounter in various forms of media. Encouraging open conversations about body image, self-worth, and gender expectations can also be incredibly empowering. Additionally, seeking support from mental health professionals can help individuals navigate the emotional challenges associated with the Toxic Female Gaze.

Interview 2: Dr. Maria Chen - Media Studies Scholar

Dr. Maria Chen specializes in media studies, focusing on the representation of gender and the impact of media on society. She has authored several books on the subject.

Q: Dr. Chen, how does media contribute to the perpetuation of the Toxic Female Gaze?

Dr. Chen: Media plays a pivotal role in shaping societal perceptions and ideals, including those related to gender. The portrayal of women in media, from advertising to film and television, often reinforces harmful stereotypes.

Women are frequently objectified, reduced to their physical appearances, and portrayed in passive or submissive roles. This not only affects how women are perceived but also influences how they perceive themselves.

Q: Are there examples of media that challenge these norms?

Dr. Chen: Absolutely. There are media producers and creators who are actively challenging these norms and pushing for more diverse and authentic representations of women. For instance, the rise of female-led and feminist-centered content is helping to counterbalance toxic portrayals. However, much work remains to be done. It's vital for consumers to support media that promotes positive female representation and to voice their demands for change.

Interview 3: Dr. Maya Rodriguez - Feminist Scholar and Activist

Dr. Maya Rodriguez is a leading feminist scholar and activist known for her work on gender equity and social justice. She is the founder of the "Equality Now" movement.

Q: Dr. Rodriguez, how can feminism contribute to dismantling the Toxic Female Gaze?

Dr. Rodriguez: Feminism is a powerful force for change in this regard. It encourages us to question the existing power structures and narratives that perpetuate the Toxic Female Gaze. Feminism seeks to empower women to define their identities and worth on their terms, not according to societal expectations. By advocating for equality and challenging harmful stereotypes, feminism can help shift the narrative surrounding women and their roles in society.

Q: What actions can individuals take to support feminist efforts in combating the Toxic Female Gaze?

Dr. Rodriguez: First and foremost, individuals can educate themselves about feminism and its principles. They can also actively support organizations and initiatives that promote gender equality and challenge the Toxic Female Gaze. Furthermore, it's crucial for individuals to engage in conversations with friends, family, and colleagues about these issues, fostering awareness and encouraging collective action.

—

These interviews provide us with valuable insights into the Toxic Female Gaze from the perspectives of psychology, media studies, and feminism. Dr. Sarah Reynolds highlights the psychological toll of this gaze, emphasizing the importance of media literacy and open dialogue. Dr. Maria Chen underscores the role of media in perpetuating harmful stereotypes and the need to support media that challenges these norms. Lastly, Dr. Maya Rodriguez highlights the transformative potential of feminism in reshaping societal narratives and calls for active engagement in gender equity efforts.

As we continue our exploration, it is clear that a multidimensional approach, drawing from psychology, media studies, feminism, and the wisdom of experts, is essential to addressing and dismantling the Toxic Female Gaze effectively. It is through this collective effort that we can aspire to a more equitable and inclusive society where women are celebrated for their authenticity and strength rather than confined by toxic ideals.

Chapter 11:
Case Studies and Personal Stories

In the previous chapters, we've explored the concept of the toxic female gaze and its profound impact on individuals and society. Now, it's time to turn our attention to the stories of those who have confronted and triumphed over these toxic ideals. Their experiences serve as powerful reminders of the strength of the human spirit and the potential for positive change.

The Power of Personal Narratives

Personal stories have an unparalleled ability to connect with readers on a deeply emotional level. They allow us to step into someone else's shoes, to feel their pain, and to share in their moments of triumph. In this chapter, we will hear from individuals who have navigated the treacherous waters of the toxic female gaze and emerged stronger, more resilient, and determined to rewrite their own narratives.

Sarah's Journey to Self-Acceptance

Sarah's story is a testament to the corrosive impact of societal beauty standards perpetuated by the media. Growing up, she was bombarded with images of flawless models and celebrities, leading her to believe that her worth hinged on her appearance. She recalls, "I felt like I had to meet these unattainable beauty ideals to be accepted."

It wasn't until her early twenties that Sarah embarked on a journey of self-discovery. She joined a support group for women struggling with body image issues and began therapy. Through these experiences, she learned to challenge the toxic messages she had internalized for so long. "I started to realize that my value wasn't determined by my weight or appearance," Sarah says. "I found strength in embracing my unique qualities and stopped comparing myself to others."

Sarah's journey is a testament to the power of self-acceptance and the importance of seeking support when facing the pressures of the toxic female gaze. Her story encourages us to question societal beauty ideals and prioritize our inner well-being.

Breaking Free from Societal Expectations - Maya's Story

Maya grew up in a traditional household where she was expected to conform to rigid gender roles. As a young girl, she was told that her primary goal in life was to find a husband and start a family. These expectations weighed heavily on her, and she often felt as though her dreams and ambitions were secondary.

In her late teens, Maya defied societal expectations by pursuing a career in engineering. She faced criticism and resistance from family and acquaintances who questioned her choices. However, Maya's determination to live life on her terms only grew stronger. "I realized that I had the right to define my own path," she says. "I didn't have to conform to anyone else's vision of who I should be."

Maya's story underscores the importance of challenging traditional gender roles and pursuing one's passions and aspirations without constraint. Her journey empowers us to question and break free from the toxic constraints imposed by society.

From Victim to Survivor - Lisa's Experience

Lisa's story is one of resilience in the face of adversity. She survived an emotionally abusive relationship where she was constantly belittled and made to feel inadequate. The toxic female gaze in this context manifested as a partner who sought to control and undermine her self-esteem.

Leaving the relationship was not easy for Lisa, but with the support of friends, family, and therapy, she began the process of healing and rebuilding her self-worth. "I had to learn that I deserved better," she shares. "I reclaimed my identity and realized that I could define my own worth."

Lisa's journey from victim to survivor is a testament to the strength and resilience that can be found within. Her story reminds us that it's never too late to break free from toxic relationships and regain control of our lives.

Overcoming Stereotypes in the Workplace - Maria's Triumph

Maria faced the double bind of workplace stereotypes associated with the toxic female gaze. As a leader in a male-dominated industry, she encountered resistance from colleagues and superiors who questioned her competence and leadership abilities based on her gender.

Rather than succumb to these stereotypes, Maria embraced her unique leadership style, which emphasized empathy, collaboration, and inclusivity. Over time, she not only earned the respect of her peers but also paved the way for more inclusive leadership practices within her organization.

Maria's story illustrates how women can shatter workplace stereotypes by staying true to their values and forging a path that challenges the status quo. Her journey inspires us to overcome obstacles and embrace our strengths, even in the face of bias.

–

These personal stories are just a glimpse into the diverse and powerful experiences of individuals who have confronted and conquered the toxic female gaze. Each story underscores the importance of self-acceptance, resilience, and the capacity for positive change.

In the final chapters of this book, we will delve into practical strategies for breaking free from the toxic female gaze and promoting a more inclusive and empowering narrative for women. These strategies are informed by the lessons learned from these personal narratives, offering readers a roadmap to navigate their own journeys toward self-discovery and empowerment.

"In the second box office year impacted by the pandemic, female characters accounted for 35% of major characters in the top 100 grossing films... Females comprised 34% of all speaking characters... 85% of films featured more male than female characters. Only 7% of films had more female than male characters, and 8% of films featured equal numbers of female and male characters"

Chapter 12:
Legal and Policy Considerations

In our exploration of the toxic female gaze, it is essential to delve into the legal and policy dimensions that both perpetuate and combat this pervasive issue. Laws and policies play a significant role in shaping societal norms and behaviors, and they can either reinforce harmful stereotypes or work towards dismantling them. This chapter examines the legal and policy considerations surrounding the toxic female gaze, shedding light on the progress made and the challenges that persist.

Section 1: Gender Discrimination Laws

Gender discrimination is a fundamental issue that intersects with the toxic female gaze. Various countries have enacted laws aimed at preventing gender-based discrimination in areas such as employment, education, and public accommodations. These laws seek to address inequalities that arise from the toxic female gaze and provide legal recourse for individuals who experience discrimination.

Title IX and Education: In the United States, Title IX of the Education Amendments of 1972 prohibits sex-based discrimination in federally funded education programs. This law has been instrumental in challenging gender stereotypes and promoting equal opportunities for women in education.

Equal Pay Legislation: Many countries have introduced legislation addressing the gender pay gap, which is closely linked to the toxic female gaze's devaluation of women's contributions. These laws aim to ensure that women are paid fairly for their work and that pay disparities are addressed.

Section 2: Workplace Policies and Initiatives

Workplaces are often breeding grounds for the toxic female gaze, where women may face biases, stereotypes, and unequal treatment. To counteract these issues, organizations can implement policies and initiatives designed to create more inclusive and equitable environments.

Gender Diversity Initiatives: Many companies are adopting gender diversity initiatives to promote the inclusion of women in leadership positions and decision-making roles. These initiatives challenge traditional gender norms and foster a more balanced representation in the workplace.

Anti-Harassment Policies: Robust anti-harassment policies are crucial for combating the toxic female gaze's impact on workplace culture. These policies send a clear message that harassment and discrimination will not be tolerated.

Section 3: Intersectionality and the Law

The toxic female gaze affects individuals differently based on their intersecting identities, such as race, sexuality, and disability. Legal frameworks must consider these intersecting factors to address the unique challenges faced by different groups of women.

Intersectional Approaches: Advocates and policymakers are increasingly recognizing the importance of intersectionality in addressing gender discrimination. Laws and policies are evolving to consider the multiple dimensions of identity that women may experience.

Section 4: Challenges and Gaps

While progress has been made in addressing the toxic female gaze through legal and policy measures, significant challenges and gaps remain.

Enforcement and Awareness: In many cases, existing laws and policies are not effectively enforced, and individuals may not be aware of their rights. Education and awareness campaigns are essential to ensuring that women understand their legal protections.

Online Spaces and Cyberbullying: The digital age has introduced new challenges related to the toxic female gaze, including online harassment and cyberbullying. Laws and policies must adapt to address these evolving forms of discrimination.

Section 5: The Role of Advocacy

Advocacy groups and activists have played a crucial role in pushing for legal and policy changes that combat the toxic female gaze. These efforts have led to important legislative victories and increased awareness of the issue.

#MeToo Movement: The #MeToo movement, which began in 2017, highlighted the prevalence of sexual harassment and assault and led to significant discussions around changing laws and workplace policies.

Global Advocacy: International organizations and grassroots movements around the world are working to address the toxic female gaze on a global scale. The Convention on the Elimination of All Forms of Discrimination Against Women (CEDAW) is one example of a global effort to combat gender-based discrimination.

Section 6: Future Directions

As we look ahead, there are several key directions that legal and policy considerations can take to address the toxic female gaze more effectively.

Comprehensive Legislation: Comprehensive legislation that explicitly addresses the toxic female gaze and its consequences may be necessary to provide a stronger legal framework for combating these issues.

Data Collection and Research: More research and data collection efforts are needed to better understand the prevalence and impact of the toxic female gaze in various contexts. This information can inform the development of evidence-based policies.

Legal and policy considerations are essential aspects of addressing the toxic female gaze. While progress has been made, challenges persist, and ongoing advocacy and activism are necessary to drive meaningful change. By working together at the intersection of law, policy, and advocacy, we can strive for a future where the toxic female gaze holds no power, and all individuals are treated with dignity and respect, regardless of their gender.

Chapter 13:
Policy Recommendations

In the preceding chapters, we've delved deep into the concept of the toxic female gaze, exploring its origins, manifestations, and the profound impact it has on individuals and society. Now, as we conclude our journey, it is crucial to shift our focus towards actionable solutions and policy recommendations that can help dismantle this toxic framework and pave the way for a more equitable future.

Understanding the Role of Policy

Policy plays a pivotal role in shaping societal norms and behaviors. It provides a framework for how institutions, organizations, and governments interact with individuals and communities. Therefore, addressing the toxic female gaze at a systemic level requires comprehensive policy changes and initiatives. Here are some key policy recommendations:

1. Education Reform

Policy Recommendation: Implement Comprehensive Gender Education Programs

Rationale: To combat the toxic female gaze, we must start early by educating the next generation about gender stereotypes, biases, and healthy relationships. Comprehensive gender education programs should be integrated into school curricula, covering topics such as media literacy, consent, body image, and gender equality.

2. Media Representation

Policy Recommendation: Establish Media Accountability and Diversity Standards

Rationale: Media plays a significant role in perpetuating toxic female gaze stereotypes. Governments and regulatory bodies should work with media outlets to establish and enforce standards for diversity and fair representation. Encourage the creation and promotion of content that reflects the true diversity of women's experiences.

3. Workplace Equality

Policy Recommendation: Enforce Gender Equality Legislation

Rationale: Governments should enforce stringent gender equality legislation, ensuring equal pay for equal work and promoting inclusive hiring practices. Implement policies that support parental leave and flexible work arrangements to alleviate the pressures women often face due to societal expectations.

4. Mental Health Support

Policy Recommendation: Expand Access to Mental Health Services

Rationale: Recognizing the detrimental impact of the toxic female gaze on mental health, governments should prioritize mental health services and support networks, making them accessible and affordable to all. These services should include counseling and therapy programs that address body image issues, self-esteem, and resilience.

5. Representation in Leadership

Policy Recommendation: Implement Gender Quotas in Leadership Positions

Rationale: To break the cycle of the toxic female gaze in positions of power and influence, governments and organizations should consider implementing gender quotas. This ensures that women have a fair chance to occupy leadership roles in politics, business, and other fields.

6. Social Media Regulations

Policy Recommendation: Regulate Social Media Platforms

Rationale: Social media platforms have become breeding grounds for the toxic female gaze. Governments should work with tech companies to establish regulations that curb harmful content, hate speech, and online harassment. Promote media literacy programs to help users critically engage with online content.

7. Support for Marginalized Communities

Policy Recommendation: Invest in Intersectional Initiatives

Rationale: Recognize that the impact of the toxic female gaze varies based on intersectionality. Develop policies and programs that specifically address the unique challenges faced by marginalized communities, including women of color, LGBTQ+ individuals, and those with disabilities.

8. Research and Data Collection

Policy Recommendation: Fund Research on Gender and Media

Rationale: Support research initiatives that examine the evolving nature of the toxic female gaze, its consequences, and potential solutions. Use data-driven insights to inform policy decisions and track progress over time.

9. Public Awareness Campaigns

Policy Recommendation: Launch National Awareness Campaigns

Rationale: Governments should collaborate with advocacy groups to launch national campaigns that raise awareness about the toxic female gaze. These campaigns should challenge stereotypes, promote body positivity, and encourage healthy relationships.

10. Collaboration and Accountability

Policy Recommendation: Foster Cross-Sector Collaboration

Rationale: Encourage collaboration between government bodies, civil society organizations, media, and the private sector to address the toxic female gaze comprehensively. Create mechanisms for ongoing monitoring and accountability to ensure that policies are effective.

Addressing the toxic female gaze at a policy level is not only a moral imperative but also an essential step toward a more equitable and inclusive society. These policy recommendations are not exhaustive but serve as a starting point for the systemic changes needed to dismantle harmful stereotypes and empower women to define their identities on their own terms.

Let us remember that change is possible, and it begins with awareness, education, and collective action. It is our hope that this book will ignite a spark within you to advocate for these policy changes and be part of the movement toward a world where the toxic female gaze no longer holds sway, and all individuals can live authentically and free from harmful societal pressures.

They are, in a sense, two sides of the same coin: women are, on the one hand, subjects of an extremely real and abject (as Julia Kristeva put it) body and denigrated sexuality; on the other, the proliferation of images, and their digitalisation produces more and more abstract and air-brushed representations of impossible female bodies. Both indicate, certainly, a "lack of progress." But, one hopes, discussions and resistance are emerging in response.

- Laura Mulvey

Chapter 14:
Global Perspectives

The toxic female gaze is not limited to any one culture of geographical region; it is a phenomenon that transcends borders, affecting women and gender minorities worldwide. In this chapter, we will explore global perspectives on the toxic female gaze, examining how it manifests differently in various cultures and regions while also acknowledging commonalities in its impact.

Cultural Nuances

Each culture has its own set of expectations, norms, and stereotypes surrounding femininity. These cultural nuances significantly influence the way the toxic female gaze operates.

In some cultures, beauty standards may emphasize fair skin, while in others, a specific body shape or size is deemed ideal. These ideals are perpetuated through media, advertising, and societal pressures, leading to the toxic female gaze's manifestation in different forms.

For example, in South Korea, there is a phenomenon known as "K-beauty" that places immense pressure on women to achieve flawless, youthful skin and adhere to specific beauty rituals. This not only impacts self-esteem but also contributes to the normalization of invasive beauty procedures.

Intersectionality

Global perspectives on the toxic female gaze must also consider intersectionality, recognizing that the experience of the gaze varies significantly depending on an individual's race, ethnicity, sexual orientation, and socioeconomic status.

For instance, women in the Middle East may face distinct challenges related to the intersection of the toxic female gaze and cultural norms. In some countries, strict dress codes and gender segregation reinforce traditional gender roles, making it difficult for women to break free from the toxic gaze's expectations.

In contrast, women of color in Western societies may contend with racialized beauty standards that compound the pressures they experience. Media representations often favor Eurocentric features, leading to feelings of inadequacy and exclusion among those who do not fit this mold.

Local Activism

Despite these challenges, there are countless individuals and grassroots movements working to challenge and reshape the toxic female gaze in their respective communities.

In India, the "Dark is Beautiful" campaign emerged to challenge colorism and promote the beauty of diverse skin tones. This movement has sparked conversations about beauty standards and discrimination, encouraging self-acceptance among women of all backgrounds.

Similarly, in Mexico, the "Redefine Beauty" movement has gained momentum, advocating for body positivity and inclusivity in the media. By showcasing women of different shapes, sizes, and abilities, this movement aims to challenge the narrow beauty ideals that have long dominated Mexican society.

Global Solidarity

While the toxic female gaze may manifest differently across cultures, there is a growing sense of global solidarity among individuals and organizations working to combat it. The power of social media and digital connectivity has allowed for the exchange of ideas and the creation of international networks of support.

The #MeToo movement, for instance, transcended borders and languages to bring attention to issues of harassment and discrimination faced by women worldwide. It demonstrated that the toxic female gaze is not isolated to any one culture but is a pervasive issue that unites women in their pursuit of justice and equality.

Challenges and Progress

It is important to acknowledge that progress is not uniform across the globe. While some countries have made strides in challenging the toxic female gaze through policy changes and social movements, others continue to grapple with deeply entrenched gender stereotypes and discrimination.

In Saudi Arabia, for example, there have been recent reforms aimed at expanding women's rights and opportunities. However, women in the country still face significant challenges, including restrictions on their mobility and autonomy.

—

This chapter highlights the global nature of the toxic female gaze and the diverse ways in which it affects women and gender minorities worldwide. While cultural nuances and intersectional factors shape the experience, there is a shared sense of resilience and determination among those working to challenge and redefine societal norms.

Understanding these global perspectives is crucial for developing a comprehensive approach to addressing the toxic female gaze. By recognizing both the unique challenges faced by individuals in different cultures and the common threads that bind their experiences, we can work toward a more inclusive and equitable world where the toxic female gaze loses its power.

"There's something different about when a female directs versus a male. The level of maturity, mutual respect, and energy that you get from a female director is so different. I've worked with male directors who aren't good, and no one says anything about it, but then we had one female director who was kind of all over the place and everyone complained. It's so gendered. I feel safer when working with a female director because I know it's from a female gaze."

— Rowan Blanchard

Chapter 15:
A Vision for the Future: Celebrating Authenticity in the Female Gaze

In this final chapter, we take a leap into the future, imagining a world where the female gaze transforms into a force for good. We envision a society that values authenticity and empowers everyone to embrace their true selves. While it may seem like an ambitious goal, it is one that can guide us towards a more inclusive and accepting world.

1. Rewriting the Narrative

Defying Stereotypes: In this section, we explore how artists, writers, filmmakers, and creators are challenging traditional stereotypes associated with the female gaze. We delve into examples of media that promote diverse, complex, and authentic representations of women.

Fostering Empathy: We discuss how media and storytelling can be used to build empathy by sharing diverse narratives. We highlight projects that encourage audiences to step into the shoes of characters from different backgrounds and experiences.

2. Empowering the Next Generation

Education and Media Literacy: We explore the importance of media literacy programs that equip young people with the skills to critically analyze media portrayals. We also discuss the role of education in promoting gender equality and dismantling toxic stereotypes.

Role Models and Mentorship: We showcase the significance of female role models and mentorship programs in inspiring the next generation to pursue their dreams, irrespective of societal expectations.

3. Intersectionality and Inclusivity

Embracing Intersectionality: We emphasize the importance of intersectionality in our vision for the future. By acknowledging and celebrating the diversity of women's experiences across race, sexuality, disability, and more, we aim to create a more inclusive female gaze.

Amplifying Marginalized Voices: We highlight initiatives that amplify the voices of marginalized women and non-binary individuals, ensuring their stories and perspectives are heard and valued.

4. Nurturing Authenticity

Self-Acceptance: We discuss strategies and practices for fostering self-acceptance and self-love, encouraging individuals to embrace their authentic selves without fear of judgment.

Cultivating Confidence: We explore how confidence-building programs and support networks can help individuals break free from the constraints of the toxic female gaze and step into their power.

5. Taking Action

Advocacy and Activism: We examine how advocacy and activism play a pivotal role in transforming the female gaze. We provide examples of organizations and movements that are driving change and invite readers to get involved.

Small Steps, Big Impact: We emphasize that every individual can contribute to this vision for the future, even through small acts of kindness, empathy, and conscious media consumption.

In our vision for the future, the female gaze becomes a beacon of empowerment and authenticity. It is a gaze that celebrates diversity, embraces intersectionality, and uplifts marginalized voices. It is a force for good, inspiring individuals to break free from the confines of toxic expectations and boldly be themselves. While the journey ahead may be challenging, it is a path worth pursuing—one that leads to a more inclusive, compassionate, and authentic world for all. Together, we can shape the future of the female gaze and make this vision a reality.

I am not sure that there has been a "lack of progress." On the contrary, the concept of feminism is not only well established but is now also attracting interest from young women, including teenagers and pre-teens. But a new interest is also symptomatic of the failure of the feminist project and the need for its renewal.

- Laura Mulvey

Chapter 16:
The Future of the Female Gaze

The toxic female gaze has been a persistent issue in our society for decades, but the future holds promise for change. In this chapter, we will explore the potential transformations in the portrayal of the female gaze and how inclusivity can reshape it for the better.

Shifting the Narrative

The portrayal of the female gaze in media and society has evolved over time, reflecting changing cultural norms and values. As we move forward, there is hope for a significant shift in the narrative surrounding the female gaze. One notable development is the growing awareness and recognition of the harmful effects of toxic portrayals of women.

Media outlets, filmmakers, and content creators are increasingly facing criticism for perpetuating harmful stereotypes and toxic ideals. The #MeToo movement and similar initiatives have brought issues of gender equality, harassment, and gender-based discrimination to the forefront of public consciousness. As a result, there is a heightened awareness of the responsibility that media and entertainment industries bear in shaping public perceptions.

Many creators and industry leaders are taking steps to rectify this issue. Some are actively seeking out diverse voices and perspectives, both in front of and behind the camera. This commitment to diversity and inclusivity is a positive sign for the future of the female gaze. As the industry becomes more representative, the portrayal of women in media is likely to become more nuanced, authentic, and empowering.

Promoting Inclusivity

Inclusivity is a key factor in reshaping the female gaze. It's essential to recognize that the toxic female gaze affects women differently based on various intersecting factors, including race, sexuality, age, and socioeconomic status. Therefore, addressing the issue comprehensively requires an intersectional approach.

1. **Intersectionality:** Intersectionality acknowledges that the experiences of women are shaped by the interplay of multiple identities. For example, a Black woman's experience of the female gaze may differ significantly from that of a white woman. By understanding and addressing these differences, we can create a more inclusive and accurate representation of the female gaze.

2. **Representation Matters:** The media has a crucial role to play in promoting inclusivity. When people from diverse backgrounds are involved in the creation and production of media content, it is more likely to reflect a broader range of perspectives. This, in turn, helps challenge stereotypes and reshape the female gaze.

3. **Education and Advocacy:** Promoting inclusivity also involves education and advocacy. Schools, organizations, and community groups can play a role in raising awareness about the toxic female gaze and its impact on different communities. Advocacy efforts can lead to policy changes and industry guidelines that promote inclusivity.

4. Consumer Influence: As consumers of media, we have the power to influence the industry. By supporting media that portrays the female gaze in a positive and inclusive manner and boycotting content that perpetuates toxic stereotypes, we can send a strong message to content creators.

5. Mentorship and Empowerment: Empowering women and underrepresented groups to take on leadership roles in media and entertainment is another crucial step. Mentorship programs and initiatives that support emerging talent can help diversify the industry and ensure that more voices are heard.

The future of the female gaze is not set in stone. It is shaped by the collective efforts of individuals, communities, and industries. While the toxic female gaze has been a persistent issue, there is hope for positive change. By recognizing the problem, promoting inclusivity, and actively working toward a more diverse and authentic representation of women, we can contribute to a future where the female gaze empowers and inspires rather than restricts and objectifies. It's a future where authenticity and inclusivity prevail, creating a more equitable and just society for all.

In a world ordered by sexual imbalance, pleasure in looking has been split between active/male and passive/female...In their traditional exhibitionist role women are simultaneously looked at and displayed, with their appearance coded for strong visual and erotic impact so that they can be said to connote to-be-looked-at-ness

- Laura Mulvey

Afterword

In the journey we've embarked upon through the pages of this book, we've delved deep into the complex and often troubling terrain of the toxic female gaze. We've explored its historical roots, dissected its manifestations in the media, dissected its influence on personal relationships, and sought solutions for fostering authenticity and empowerment in the face of this pervasive phenomenon. As we conclude this exploration, it's imperative to reflect on what we've learned and how we can apply these insights to create a more inclusive, just, and authentic world.

Throughout this journey, we've uncovered the sobering reality that the toxic female gaze is not merely a modern construct but rather a culmination of centuries of ingrained societal expectations and stereotypes. It has shaped and continues to shape our perceptions of women, their roles, and their worth. The media, in its many forms, plays a substantial role in perpetuating these stereotypes, often reducing women to two-dimensional, harmful caricatures. The consequences of this are not confined to the screen but reverberate into our personal lives, influencing how we perceive ourselves and others.

Yet, despite these challenges, we must not succumb to despair.

This book has been about more than merely illuminating the problems. It's been about inspiring change, challenging the status quo, and empowering individuals to embrace their authenticity unapologetically. The toxic female gaze, though deeply rooted, is not an insurmountable obstacle. It can be dismantled, and its toxic elements can be replaced with a healthier, more inclusive vision of womanhood.

Breaking Free from Toxicity

The path to dismantling the toxic female gaze begins with self-awareness and introspection. It necessitates recognizing the harmful patterns and stereotypes that we've internalized or perpetuated in our own lives. It entails questioning our own biases, judgments, and expectations. It demands that we examine the media we consume critically and be discerning consumers who demand more diverse and authentic representations.

In our discussions about toxic femininity, we've explored how societal pressure can lead women to conform to harmful ideals, stifling their individuality and authentic selves. However, we've also celebrated the resilience of individuals who have broken free from these constraints, showcasing how embracing one's true self can lead to a more fulfilling and empowered life.

Toxic femininity isn't about blaming women for perpetuating these ideals. It's about understanding the systemic forces at play and the ways in which they've shaped our behaviors and choices. By fostering an environment of compassion and self-acceptance, we can support each other in our journeys towards authenticity.

Fostering Positive Female Empowerment

True empowerment arises when women are encouraged to embrace their multifaceted identities, free from the limitations of the toxic female gaze. It's about recognizing that there is no single "right" way to be a woman. Empowerment is found in the celebration of diversity, in the acknowledgment that each woman's narrative is unique and valid.

Throughout this book, we've spotlighted inspiring initiatives, movements, and individuals who are at the forefront of reshaping the narrative surrounding the female gaze. These pioneers have been instrumental in challenging the status quo and pushing for more inclusive, authentic portrayals of women.

Empowerment also involves nurturing a sense of agency and self-determination. It means equipping women with the tools and knowledge they need to navigate the world confidently. Education, mentorship, and access to resources are vital in this regard. It's incumbent upon us as a society to ensure that these opportunities are available to all, regardless of gender, race, or socioeconomic status.

The Future of the Female Gaze

As we wrap up our exploration, it's natural to wonder about the future. What lies ahead in our ongoing quest to redefine and reclaim the female gaze?

Change is already underway. The media landscape is shifting, albeit gradually, towards more inclusive and authentic representations of women. We've seen a growing recognition of the need for diversity in storytelling and the importance of intersectionality. As more voices are heard, and as more individuals demand change, the media has begun to respond.

But the future also depends on each of us. It hinges on our commitment to challenging toxic elements when we encounter them, whether in the media, in our personal relationships, or within ourselves. It's about amplifying the voices of those who have long been marginalized and supporting initiatives that promote inclusivity and authenticity.

Moreover, the future of the female gaze is a collective endeavor. It's about fostering empathy and solidarity among all genders, recognizing that dismantling harmful stereotypes benefits everyone. We must encourage open dialogue and engage in constructive conversations about gender roles, expectations, and the evolving nature of womanhood.

In the face of the toxic female gaze, we have a choice. We can perpetuate the status quo or be the architects of change. We can choose to embrace authenticity, celebrate diversity, and empower individuals to break free from the constraints of harmful stereotypes. The toxic female gaze may be deeply ingrained, but it is not immutable. Together, we have the power to redefine the narrative, foster inclusivity, and create a world where every woman can be her authentic self without fear or judgment.

The journey we've undertaken through these pages is not the end but rather the beginning of a transformative process. It's an invitation to take what we've learned and apply it to our lives, to our communities, and to the world at large. It's an opportunity to be agents of change, champions of authenticity, and advocates for a more equitable and just society—one where the toxic female gaze is replaced with a vision of womanhood that celebrates the beautiful tapestry of human diversity.

Discussion and Reflection

In our journey to understand the intricacies of the toxic female gaze, we've explored its historical roots, its manifestation in various aspects of society, and the impact it has on individuals and relationships. Now, it's time to turn the spotlight onto you, the reader, and invite you to engage with the material on a deeper level. In this chapter, we'll provide a series of thought-provoking discussion questions and exercises designed to encourage reflection, conversation, and action.

Discussion Questions: Challenging the Status Quo

1. Self-Reflection: How have societal expectations influenced your own perception of femininity and the female gaze? Can you identify any toxic elements in your beliefs or behaviors?

2. Media Influence: Think about the media you consume regularly, including TV shows, movies, and magazines. How do these sources contribute to or challenge the toxic female gaze? Are there specific portrayals or advertisements that have left a lasting impact on you?

3. Intersectionality: Consider how race, sexuality, and other aspects of identity intersect with the toxic female gaze. How do these intersections affect individuals' experiences of toxic femininity?

4. Education and Awareness: What steps can you take to educate yourself and raise awareness about the toxic female gaze? How can you promote discussions about this topic within your community or social circles?

5. Supportive Relationships: Reflect on your personal relationships. Are there ways in which you or your loved ones perpetuate toxic elements of the female gaze? How can you foster healthier, more authentic connections?

Exercises: Taking Action

6. Media Consumption Audit: Spend a week documenting the media you consume, paying close attention to portrayals of femininity and the female gaze. Afterward, analyze your findings and consider whether you want to make any changes to your media diet.

7. Writing Your Narrative: Write a personal essay or journal entry that explores your own experiences with the female gaze. How have these experiences shaped your identity and relationships? What steps can you take to reclaim your narrative?

8. Conversations with Others: Engage in open and empathetic conversations with friends and family members about the toxic female gaze. Share what you've learned and encourage them to reflect on their own beliefs and behaviors.

9. Supporting Positive Representation: Identify organizations, movements, or initiatives that promote positive and diverse representations of femininity. Consider volunteering, donating, or advocating for these causes.

10. Action Plan: Develop a personal action plan that outlines concrete steps you can take to challenge and combat the toxic female gaze in your life. Set goals and deadlines to hold yourself accountable.

Sharing and Learning Together

Remember that discussions about the toxic female gaze are not meant to place blame or create guilt but rather to promote awareness and inspire positive change. By engaging with these questions and exercises, you're taking the first steps toward fostering a healthier and more authentic perception of femininity, both within yourself and within society.

Additionally, consider joining or starting a book club or discussion group focused on topics related to gender, feminism, and media literacy. Sharing your insights and experiences with others can be a powerful way to learn, grow, and effect change collectively.

I want to emphasize that tackling the toxic female gaze is an ongoing process. It requires self-reflection, open dialogue, and a commitment to challenging harmful stereotypes and expectations. By actively engaging with the material in this book and by fostering discussions within your community, you can contribute to a more inclusive and empowering world for all individuals, regardless of gender.

Empowering Authenticity Through Interactive Exercises

In this book, we've explored the concept of the toxic female gaze, dissecting its origins, manifestations, and consequences. Now, it's time to embark on a journey of self-reflection and empowerment. In this chapter, we'll engage in interactive exercises designed to help you recognize and challenge the toxic elements of the female gaze, fostering a deeper understanding of yourself and the world around you.

Exercise 1: The Mirror of Self-Reflection

Objective: To examine and reflect on your personal beliefs and attitudes about femininity and the female gaze.

Instructions:

1. Find a quiet and comfortable space where you won't be interrupted.

2. Take a few deep breaths to center yourself and clear your mind.

3. Look in the mirror, and as you do, ask yourself the following questions:
 - How do I perceive my own femininity?
 - What societal expectations or beauty standards have influenced my self-image?
 - Have I ever felt pressure to conform to a particular image of femininity?

4. Without judgment, write down your thoughts and feelings in a journal or on a piece of paper. Be honest and open with yourself.

5. Afterward, review your reflections. Are there any patterns or recurring themes that stand out? Take note of them.

6. Consider how these reflections relate to the toxic female gaze. Are there aspects of your self-perception that have been influenced by harmful stereotypes or unrealistic ideals? What steps can you take to redefine your own sense of femininity on your terms?

Exercise 2: The Media Detox Challenge

Objective: To assess and reduce the impact of media on your perceptions of femininity.

Instructions:

1. Over the next week, keep a media diary. Record the types of media you consume, including television shows, movies, magazines, social media platforms, and websites.

2. As you consume media, pay attention to the way women are portrayed. Note any instances of objectification, unrealistic beauty standards, or harmful stereotypes.

3. At the end of the week, review your diary entries. What trends or patterns do you notice in the portrayal of women in the media you consume?

4. Select one media source or platform that you feel has a particularly negative influence on your perceptions of femininity.

5. Challenge yourself to take a one-week break from that specific media source. During this time, explore alternative media that promotes healthier and more authentic representations of women.

6. After the week-long media detox, reflect on how it has affected your perceptions and self-esteem. Did you notice any positive changes? How can you continue to make conscious media choices that support a healthier view of femininity?

Exercise 3: The Empathy Walk

Objective: To develop empathy and understanding for the experiences of others who may be affected by the toxic female gaze.

Instructions:

1. Choose a day to embark on an "Empathy Walk." This exercise is most effective when done in a public space where you can observe a diverse range of people.

2. As you walk, make a conscious effort to observe and empathize with the people you encounter. Consider the diverse backgrounds, experiences, and challenges that each person may face.

3. Pay special attention to women and how they present themselves. Are there instances where you can identify signs of insecurity, self–consciousness, or attempts to conform to societal expectations of femininity?

4. Reflect on your observations during the walk. How did it feel to step into the shoes of an empathetic observer? What insights did you gain about the experiences of women who may grapple with the toxic female gaze?

5. Use this newfound empathy to engage in more supportive and understanding conversations with the women in your life. Encourage them to share their experiences and feelings, creating a safe space for open dialogue.

–

These interactive exercises are just the beginning of your journey toward recognizing and challenging the toxic female gaze. They are meant to encourage introspection, critical thinking, and empathy as you navigate the complexities of femininity and its societal expectations. Remember that change starts with self-awareness and small, intentional steps toward empowerment and authenticity.

Dear Reader,

Thank you for choosing to explore "The Toxic Female Gaze" We hope you've found this book insightful and empowering on your journey toward sustainable wellness. Your feedback is invaluable to us, and we would greatly appreciate your thoughts in the form of a book review.

Your review can help other readers discover the book and make informed decisions about their own path to health. Whether you loved it, had mixed feelings, or encountered challenges, your honest opinion matters.

Here are some questions to consider when writing your review:

1. What were your key takeaways from the book?
2. How has "The Toxic Female Gaze" influenced your perspective on health and well-being?
3. Did you find the practical strategies and advice provided in the book helpful?
4. Were there any specific moments or insights that resonated with you?
5. How has the book impacted your daily life and habits?
6. Would you recommend this book to others, and if so, why?

Your review can be as brief or detailed as you'd like, and your unique perspective is what makes it valuable. Simply click on the "Write a Review" button and share your thoughts with fellow readers.

Thank you for taking the time to share your feedback and for being a part of our community committed to lasting health and vitality. Your review will contribute to the ongoing conversation and inspire others to embark on their own transformative journeys.

With gratitude,

Liz Fe Lifestyle
The Author and Publisher of "The Toxic Female Gaze"

Appendix

In this appendix, you'll find a wealth of additional resources and acknowledgments that will further enrich your understanding of the "Toxic Female Gaze" and recognize the invaluable contributions of those who helped bring this book to fruition.

Additional Resources

1. Books

- "The Second Sex" by Simone de Beauvoir: A seminal work on women's oppression and societal expectations.
- "Composing a Life" by Mary Catherine Bateson: Exploring the intersection of gender, identity, and personal narratives.
- "The Beauty Myth" by Naomi Wolf: Analyzing the impact of beauty standards on women's lives.

2. Articles

- "The Female Gaze" by Alicia Malone: A thought-provoking article exploring the concept of the female gaze in cinema.
- "Toxic Femininity and How Patriarchy Fails Men" by Arwa Mahdawi: A critique of toxic femininity and its implications for both men and women.

3. Websites and Online Communities

   - [The Representation Project]
(https://therepresentationproject.org/): An organization dedicated
to challenging gender stereotypes in media.
   - [Everyday Feminism](https://everydayfeminism.com/): A
platform providing resources and articles on various aspects of
feminism and social justice.
   - [Bitch Media](https://www.bitchmedia.org/): A feminist media
outlet offering critical analysis of popular culture.

4. Documentaries

   - "Miss Representation": A documentary film examining the
portrayal of women in the media and its impact on society.
   - "The Mask You Live In": An exploration of how narrow
definitions of masculinity can be harmful to both men and
women.

5. Online Courses

   - [Coursera - Gender Issues and Sexuality: Essential Primary
Sources](https://www.coursera.org/learn/gender-issues-and-
sexuality): A course offering an in-depth look at gender and
sexuality through historical texts.

6. Research Papers

   - "The Influence of Media on Body Image: A Meta-Analysis of
Studies" by Grabe, S., Ward, L. M., & Hyde, J. S.: A comprehensive
analysis of media's impact on body image.

A Glossary

Understanding the dynamics of the toxic female gaze and its associated concepts often involves navigating a complex and evolving vocabulary. In this chapter, we'll provide a comprehensive glossary of key terms, phrases, and concepts related to gender studies, feminism, and the toxic female gaze. This glossary aims to enhance your comprehension of the topics discussed in this book and to empower you to engage in informed discussions surrounding these important issues.

1. Gender Binary: The traditional classification of gender into two distinct categories, male and female, based on anatomical and biological differences. It fails to acknowledge the diversity of gender identities beyond this binary, such as non-binary, genderqueer, and transgender identities.

2. Patriarchy: A social system where power and authority are primarily held by men, and male values and perspectives dominate in society. Patriarchy can perpetuate gender inequality and contribute to the toxic female gaze.

3. Intersectionality: A concept introduced by Kimberlé Crenshaw, highlighting the interconnected nature of various social identities, such as race, class, gender, and sexuality. Intersectionality recognizes that individuals may experience discrimination differently based on the convergence of these identities.

4. Toxic Masculinity: A set of harmful societal expectations and behaviors imposed on men that emphasize dominance, emotional suppression, and aggression. Toxic masculinity can interact with the toxic female gaze to reinforce harmful stereotypes.

5. Internalized Misogyny: The internalization of sexist beliefs and attitudes by individuals, including women, which leads them to devalue and discriminate against women, often unknowingly.

6. Feminism: A diverse social and political movement advocating for equal rights and opportunities for all genders. Feminism aims to challenge and dismantle gender-based discrimination and stereotypes.

7. Media Literacy: The ability to critically analyze and interpret media content, including its portrayal of gender, in order to understand how media influences perceptions and beliefs.

8. Body Positivity: A movement promoting self-acceptance and self-love, irrespective of one's body size, shape, or appearance. It challenges unrealistic beauty standards perpetuated by the media.

9. Sexualization: The objectification and reduction of individuals, particularly women, to their sexual attributes, often portrayed in a dehumanizing or demeaning manner.

10. Gaslighting: A form of emotional manipulation in which one person attempts to undermine another's reality, causing them to doubt their own perceptions and sanity.

11. Microaggressions: Subtle, often unintentional acts of discrimination or bias directed at marginalized groups, including women. Microaggressions can reinforce the toxic female gaze.

12. Stereotype Threat: The fear of confirming negative stereotypes about one's social group, which can lead to underperformance and self-doubt.

13. Media Representation: The portrayal of individuals or groups in the media, including film, television, advertising, and literature. Media representation can either challenge or reinforce stereotypes related to the toxic female gaze.

14. Self-objectification: When individuals view themselves primarily as objects of external observation, often focusing on their physical appearance to the detriment of their overall well-being.

15. Empowerment: The process of gaining self-confidence, control, and agency in one's life. Empowerment is a key goal in countering the toxic female gaze.

16. Mansplaining: A term used to describe the act of a man explaining something to a woman in a condescending or patronizing manner, typically about a topic on which she is knowledgeable.

17. Heteronormativity: The assumption that heterosexuality is the norm and the marginalization or erasure of non-heterosexual orientations in society.

18. Sexism: Discrimination or prejudice based on one's sex or gender, often resulting in unequal treatment, opportunities, or expectations for individuals based on their gender.

19. Toxic Relationships: Unhealthy relationships characterized by control, manipulation, emotional abuse, or other harmful behaviors.

20. Inclusivity: The practice of including and valuing diverse perspectives, identities, and experiences in all aspects of society, including media, workplaces, and social spaces.

This glossary is not exhaustive but serves as a starting point for navigating the complex terrain of gender studies, feminism, and the toxic female gaze. Familiarizing yourself with these terms will enable you to engage in more meaningful conversations and advocate for gender equality. As you continue to explore these concepts, remember that language is a powerful tool for change, and understanding these terms is a crucial step toward dismantling harmful stereotypes and promoting a more equitable society.

Resource Lists

In our exploration of the toxic female gaze, we've delved into its origins, manifestations, and effects on individuals and society. It's important to remember that awareness and understanding are just the first steps toward change. To empower ourselves and others to challenge and combat the toxic female gaze, we need practical resources, guidance, and support. In this chapter, we provide you with a valuable tool: resource lists.

Resources for Self-Reflection and Healing

1. Books for Self-Reflection

- "Daring Greatly" by Brené Brown: This book encourages vulnerability as a path to self-acceptance.
- "The Body Is Not an Apology" by Sonya Renee Taylor: Explore body positivity and self-love.
- "The Gifts of Imperfection" by Brené Brown: Learn to embrace your authentic self.

2. Online Communities and Support Groups

- **Reddit's r/TwoXChromosomes:** An active subreddit where women share their experiences and support each other.

- **The Mighty:** An online community for people facing various health and mental health challenges, where you can find support and stories related to self-esteem and mental well-being.

3. Therapy and Counseling

- **Psychology Today's Therapist Directory:** Search for therapists who specialize in self-esteem, body image, and gender issues in your area.
- **BetterHelp:** An online platform that provides access to licensed therapists and counselors.

Resources for Challenging Toxic Media Representations

4. Media Literacy Education

- **Media Smarts:** Offers free resources and lesson plans for educators and individuals to promote media literacy.
- **Center for Media Literacy:** Provides tools and resources to help people critically analyze media messages.

5. Media Watchdog Organizations

- **Geena Davis Institute on Gender in Media:** Focuses on gender representation in the entertainment industry and offers resources and research.
- **The Representation Project:** Dedicated to challenging gender stereotypes in media.

Resources for Promoting Inclusivity and Intersectionality

10. Intersectional Feminism

- **SisterSong:** A reproductive justice organization that centers the experiences of women of color.
- **Black Women's Blueprint:** Addresses the unique experiences of Black women and advocates for their rights.

11. LGBTQ+ Resources

- **GLAAD:** Promotes LGBTQ+ acceptance through media advocacy and resources.
- **The Trevor Project:** Offers crisis intervention and support for LGBTQ+ youth.

Resources for Legal and Policy Advocacy

12. Gender Equality Legislation

- **UN Women's Gender Equality Laws Database:** Access information on laws and policies related to gender equality worldwide.
- **American Association of University Women (AAUW):** Advocates for policies that advance gender equity in education and the workplace.

Incorporating these resources into your journey of understanding and challenging the toxic female gaze can make a substantial difference. Remember, you are not alone in this endeavor, and there are countless individuals, organizations, and communities ready to provide support and guidance.

Whether you're looking for self-help tools, ways to challenge media portrayals, or avenues for activism, these resource lists are a starting point to empower yourself and others in the pursuit of a more inclusive and equitable world.

As we conclude our exploration of the toxic female gaze, it is our hope that these resources will serve as a compass, guiding you toward self-discovery, empowerment, and positive change. Together, we can reshape the narrative and promote healthier, more authentic ideals of femininity and self-worth.

Annotated Bibliography

Understanding the toxic female gaze requires a deep dive into the wealth of research, literature, and thought-provoking discourse surrounding this topic. In this chapter, we provide an annotated bibliography of key texts that can serve as essential resources for readers interested in exploring various facets of the toxic female gaze in greater detail.

1. "The Second Sex" by Simone de Beauvoir

 - **Annotation:** Simone de Beauvoir's groundbreaking work delves into the societal construction of womanhood and the oppressive structures that shape women's lives. Her analysis of how women are "the other" in a male-dominated world is a foundational text in feminist philosophy and offers valuable insights into the historical context of the female gaze.

2. "Composing a Life" by Mary Catherine Bateson

 - **Annotation:** Mary Catherine Bateson's exploration of gender, identity, and personal narratives is a thought-provoking read for those interested in how societal expectations and cultural norms shape women's lives. She emphasizes the importance of crafting one's own narrative rather than conforming to preconceived roles.

3. "The Beauty Myth" by Naomi Wolf

- **Annotation:** In "The Beauty Myth," Naomi Wolf dissects the harmful impact of beauty standards on women's self-esteem and overall well-being. Her analysis reveals how the media perpetuates unrealistic ideals, contributing to the toxic female gaze and its consequences.

4. "Revolting Prostitutes" by Molly Smith and Juno Mac

- **Annotation:** Smith and Mac's work offers a fresh perspective on the female gaze by examining the experiences of sex workers. They challenge stereotypes and highlight the complex intersection of gender, sexuality, and economic exploitation, shedding light on the harmful consequences of societal judgments.

5. "Female Chauvinist Pigs" by Ariel Levy

- **Annotation:** Ariel Levy critically examines the phenomenon of women adopting and perpetuating the objectifying aspects of the male gaze. Her exploration of women's roles in reinforcing harmful gender stereotypes adds an important dimension to the conversation surrounding the toxic female gaze.

6. "The Female Gaze in Contemporary World Cinema" edited by Diana Holmes and Susannah Radstone

- **Annotation:** This collection of essays explores the female gaze in cinema, providing valuable insights into how women filmmakers and characters challenge traditional representations. It showcases diverse perspectives and cinematic styles that contribute to reshaping the way we view women on screen.

7. "Miss Representation" (Documentary)

 - **Annotation:** This documentary film directed by Jennifer Siebel Newsom highlights the harmful portrayals of women in media and politics. It reveals the media's role in perpetuating the toxic female gaze and advocates for greater gender equality in representation.

8. "The Mask You Live In" (Documentary)

 - **Annotation:** While primarily focused on toxic masculinity, this documentary directed by Jennifer Siebel Newsom explores how restrictive gender norms affect both men and women. It provides valuable context for understanding the interconnectedness of toxic femininity and masculinity.

9. "Gender Issues and Sexuality: Essential Primary Sources" (Coursera Course)

 - **Annotation:** This online course offers a comprehensive examination of gender and sexuality through historical texts. It provides an academic perspective on the development of gender roles and societal expectations, offering valuable context for understanding the toxic female gaze.

10. "The Influence of Media on Body Image: A Meta-Analysis of Studies" by Grabe, S., Ward, L. M., & Hyde, J. S.

 - **Annotation:** This research paper presents a meta-analysis of studies examining the impact of media on body image. It quantifies the effects of media exposure on body dissatisfaction, shedding light on the connection between media representation and the toxic female gaze.

These annotated resources provide a solid foundation for further exploration of the toxic female gaze. Whether you're interested in philosophical perspectives, cultural critiques, cinematic analyses, or academic research, these texts offer diverse insights into the complex and multifaceted nature of the topic. They serve as a starting point for those seeking to better understand and challenge the toxic elements of the female gaze in our society.

Acknowledgments

Writing a book is a collaborative effort, and I would like to express my heartfelt gratitude to those who have played a significant role in making this project a reality.

Research Contributors

- Dan: Your meticulous research and insightful contributions were invaluable in shaping the content of this book.

Editorial Team

- Amy: Your keen eye for detail and dedication to refining the manuscript were instrumental in ensuring the clarity and coherence of this work.

Beta Readers

- Sarah: Your feedback and constructive criticism helped fine-tune the narrative and make it more accessible to a wider audience.

Family and Friends

- Aunt Rosemarie: Your unwavering support and encouragement were a constant source of motivation.

Mentors and Advisors

- Alexandra: Your guidance and expertise in the field of publishing were instrumental in providing direction and depth to this exploration.

Readers and Supporters

- To all the readers who engage with this book and its ideas, thank you for your interest in this important conversation.

This book would not have been possible without the collective effort of these individuals and the countless others who contributed their time, expertise, and encouragement along the way. It is my hope that the insights and discussions within these pages will continue to inspire meaningful conversations and positive change in our understanding of the "Toxic Female Gaze" and its impact on society.

More Books to Check Out in the Feminist Theory Series

THE PROBLEM WITH THE MALE GAZE

THE SECRET OF BECOMING MENTALLY STRONG

BY
LIZ FE LIFESTYLE

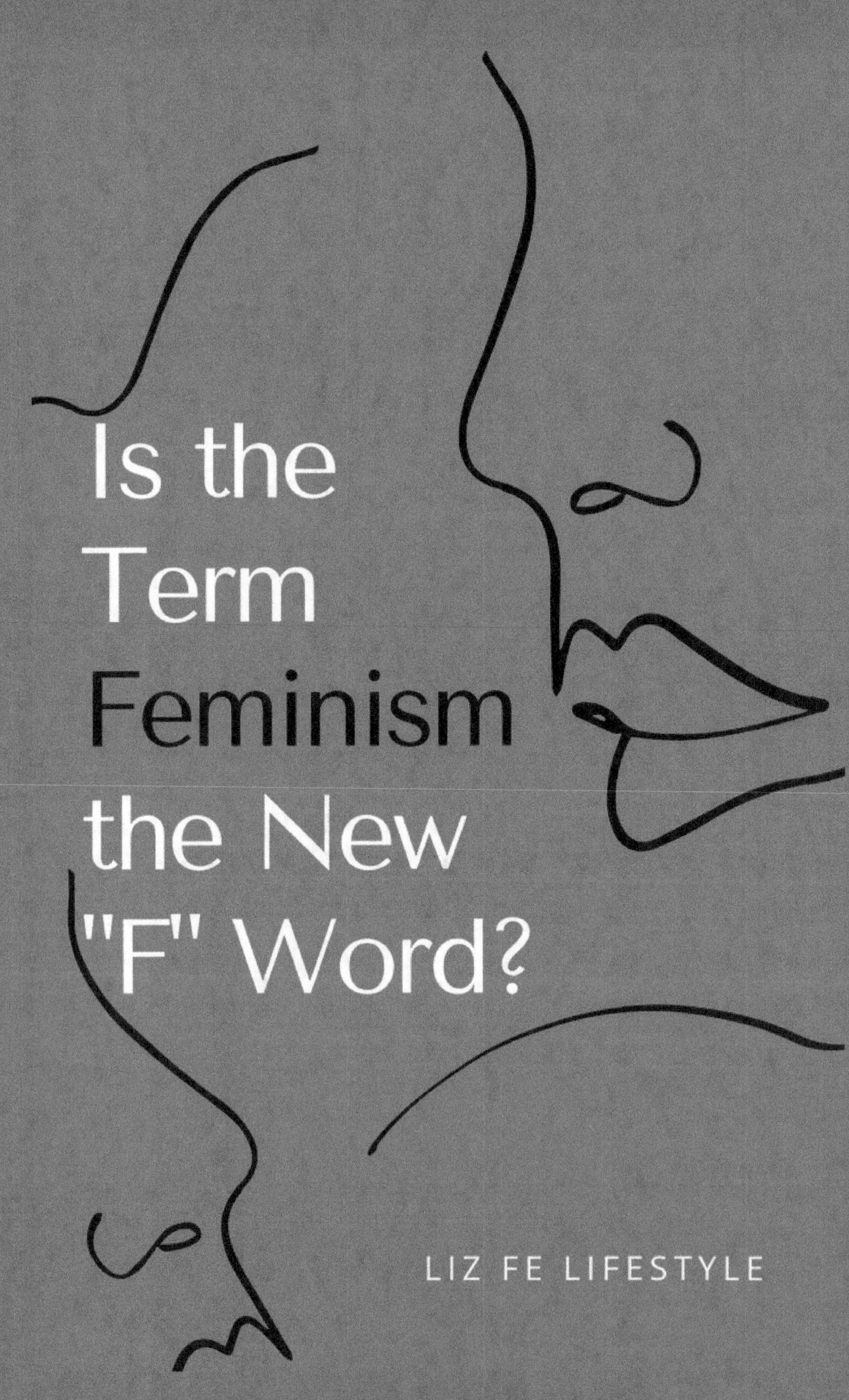
Is the
Term
Feminism
the New
"F" Word?
LIZ FE LIFESTYLE

Coming Soon

IF WOMEN DON'T OWE
MEN PRETTY, THEN
MEN
DON'T
OWE
WOMEN
MONEY
LIZ FE LIFESTYLE

WOMEN WHO HATE WOMEN

Please leave a review for us on Amazon, we really appreciate the support.

Empowered Women Book
Publisher: lizfelifestyle.com

Check Us Out: @LizFeLifestyle